Essentials of Services Marketing: Concepts, Strategies & Cases

COUNTRY PROFILES

ENGLAND

BY AMY RECHNER

BLASTOFF!
DISCOVERY

BELLWETHER MEDIA • MINNEAPOLIS, MN

Blastoff! Discovery launches a new mission: reading to learn. Filled with facts and features, each book offers you an exciting new world to explore!

This edition first published in 2018 by Bellwether Media, Inc.

No part of this publication may be reproduced in whole or in part without written permission of the publisher.
For information regarding permission, write to Bellwether Media, Inc., Attention: Permissions Department, 5357 Penn Avenue South, Minneapolis, MN 55419.

Library of Congress Cataloging-in-Publication Data

Names: Rechner, Amy, author.
Title: England / by Amy Rechner.
Description: Minneapolis, MN : Bellwether Media, Inc., 2018.
  | Series: Blastoff! Discovery: Country Profiles | Includes
  bibliographical references and index. | Audience: Grades
  3-8. | Audience: Ages 7-13.
Identifiers: LCCN 2016053600 (print) |
  LCCN 2016055569 (ebook) | ISBN 9781626176799
  (hardcover : alk. paper) | ISBN 9781681034096 (ebook)
Subjects: LCSH: England–Juvenile literature.
Classification: LCC DA27.5 .R43 2018 (print) | LCC DA27.5
  (ebook) | DDC 942–dc23
LC record available at https://lccn.loc.gov/2016053600

Library of Congress Cataloging-in-Publication Data

Editor: Christina Leaf   Designer: Brittany McIntosh

Printed in the United States of America, North Mankato, MN.

TABLE OF CONTENTS

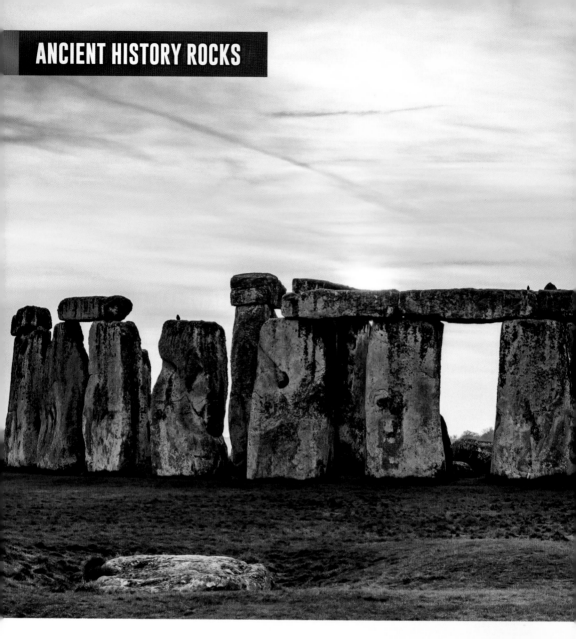

A family climbs aboard a train in a bustling London station. They are whisked from the sprawling city to the rolling hills and small villages of the countryside. In less than two hours, they reach Stonehenge. Huge slabs of ancient stone stand in the middle of a lush green field.

OTHER TOP SITES

BIG BEN

HADRIAN'S WALL

JURASSIC COAST

WINDSOR CASTLE

Everyone marvels at the mysterious site. No one knows what purpose the circle of stones once served. Nearby, a busy highway hums with traffic. Ancient countryside and modern cities live side by side here. This is England!

LOCATION

England is on the island of Great Britain, just west of **mainland** Europe. Wales borders to the west. Scotland is north. Together with Northern Ireland, these countries make up the United Kingdom. The capital of England is London. It sits in southeast England, near the division of the Eastern and Western **hemispheres**.

England covers 50,302 square miles (130,281 square kilometers). The English Channel and the North Sea separate it from the rest of Europe. The Celtic and Irish Seas lie to the west. Tiny islands dot the coasts, including the Isle of Wight.

NORTHERN IRELAND

IRELAND

CELTIC SEA

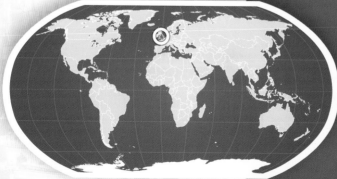

SCOTLAND

WHERE EAST MEETS WEST

Greenwich, London is where the Eastern and Western hemispheres meet. Visitors can stand with a foot in each hemisphere!

☐ = UNITED KINGDOM

NORTH SEA

LEEDS

LIVERPOOL

IRISH SEA

MANCHESTER

ENGLAND

WALES

BIRMINGHAM

LONDON

ISLE OF WIGHT

ENGLISH CHANNEL

N
W + E
S

LANDSCAPE AND CLIMATE

The **terrain** in England includes the peaks of the Cumbrian Mountains in the northwest. The Lake District, home to most of England's lakes, is nestled in the Cumbrian Mountains. The Pennines Mountains cascade through north-central England.

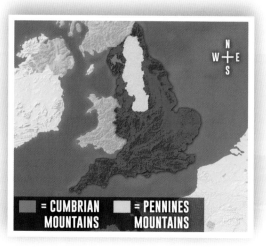

= CUMBRIAN MOUNTAINS   = PENNINES MOUNTAINS

Northeast England has bleak, windy **moors** where little grows. The moors give way to the Fens, a marshy area on the eastern shore. The Fens and the gently rolling **plains** of southern England provide good farmland.

THE WHITE CLIFFS OF DOVER

The towering cliffs of southern England glow white above the English Channel. Why white? They are made out of chalk! The cliffs near Dover are more than 300 feet (91 meters) high.

WHITE CLIFFS OF DOVER
DOVER

CAT BELLS
THE LAKE DISTRICT,
CUMBRIA

LONDON
Average
seasonal highs
and lows

JANUARY
HIGH: 43 °F (6 °C)
LOW: 36 °F (2 °C)

APRIL
HIGH: 55 °F (13 °C)
LOW: 43 °F (6 °C)

JULY
HIGH: 72 °F (22 °C)
LOW: 57 °F (14 °C)

OCTOBER
HIGH: 57 °F (14 °C)
LOW: 46 °F (8 °C)

°F = degrees Fahrenheit
°C = degrees Celsius

England's weather forecasts change quickly. Rain is common. Spring and summer bring sunshine and warmer temperatures. Winters are cold and wet, with snow and ice falling in the north.

The English countryside is a checkerboard of green fields. These fields are divided by **hedgerows**. Hedgerows shelter songbirds like finches and robins, and small animals such as mice, hedgehogs, and voles. Deer, rabbits, and foxes live in woodlands and forests.

Along England's coasts, seals sun themselves on rocks. Gulls and terns squawk overhead. Rivers are home to ducks, swans, and otters. Lamprey eels swim among the other fish.

EURASIAN BULLFINCH

VOLE

COMMON SEAL

RED FOX

A PRICKLY IDEA

In 2015, a member of Parliament called for the hedgehog to be named the national symbol of England.

MUTE SWANS

MUTE SWAN

Life Span: up to 26 years
Red List Status: least concern

mute swan range =

LEAST CONCERN	NEAR THREATENED	VULNERABLE	ENDANGERED	CRITICALLY ENDANGERED	EXTINCT IN THE WILD	EXTINCT

More than 54 million people live in England. Most of them were born there. **Immigrants** most often come from Africa, India, and the Middle East. The country's main language is English. Areas of England have different **accents**. Visitors may also have trouble understanding the local **dialects**.

Most English people are Christian. Many are Anglicans, who belong to the state Church of England. Others are Catholics. There are Muslims, Hindus, and Jewish people in England, too.

FAMOUS FACE

Name: His Royal Highness Prince Henry of Wales (Prince Harry)
Birthday: September 15, 1984
Hometown: London, England
Famous for: A popular member of Britain's royal family, and a volunteer for charities like the Invictus Games, health and education organizations in Africa, and wildlife conservation

SPEAK BRITISH ENGLISH

The English spoken in England can be very different from American English.

AMERICAN ENGLISH	BRITISH ENGLISH
backyard	garden
cookie or cracker	biscuit
french fries	chips
sweater	jumper
candy	sweets
crosswalk	zebra crossing

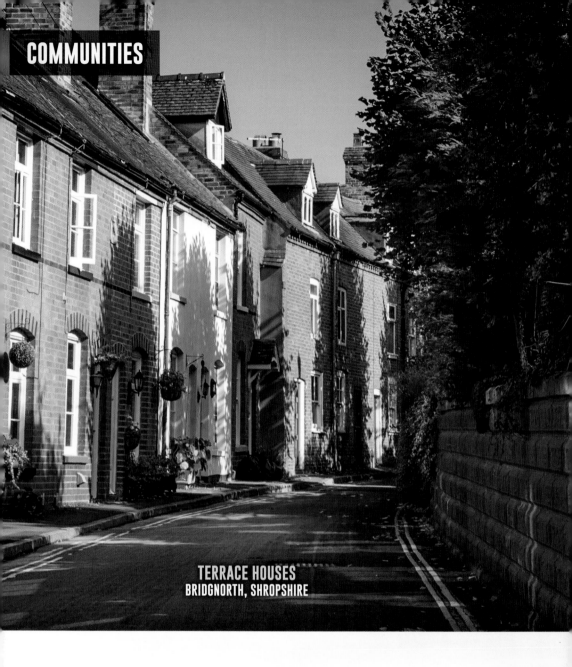

TERRACE HOUSES
BRIDGNORTH, SHROPSHIRE

The English are loyal citizens and neighbors. Cities like Birmingham or London have many close neighborhoods that feel like villages. Families are generally small, with one or two children living with one or two parents.

England's cities, towns, and countryside all have houses that are hundreds of years old. Many city dwellers live in *flats*, the British term for apartments. Terrace houses, which share walls with neighbors, are also common in cities and smaller towns. Trains connect big cities to the rest of England. Londoners ride the bus or the subway, called the Tube. Bicycling, driving, and walking are also popular.

MAGICAL PLATFORM

One of London's railway stations is King's Cross, where Harry Potter caught the Hogwarts Express. Now fans can have their pictures taken there at "Platform 9 3/4."

LIVERPOOL STREET STATION
LONDON

CUSTOMS

Good manners are an English custom. **Punctuality** is very important. "Please," "thank you," "sorry," and "excuse me" are well-used phrases. Even when outside, "indoor voices" should be used. The greatest example of English manners is the **tradition** of waiting in line. The English call it **queuing**. It is not okay to cut in line! Everyone is expected to line up neatly and patiently wait their turn.

English people are also famous for being **reserved**. It is considered proper behavior to keep emotions in check and avoid rudeness, so as not to offend others. Sometimes that is difficult while watching sports!

CAFE TEA ROOMS

QUEUING

NO EXCUSE

One word that is often heard in England is "sorry." The English use it to apologize and also to signal they did not hear something. It is all part of the wish to be polite.

English children start school when they are 5 years old. Many attend state schools, which are free and run by the government. Others go to independent schools. These cost money, and students must apply to be able to attend. At age 16, students are done with the basics of schooling. However, most choose to remain until age 18 to better prepare for trade school, **apprenticeships**, or college.

Most jobs in England are **service jobs**. Those include banking, insurance, and **tourism**. Manufacturing, farming, and fishing are also important industries. English farmers raise more livestock than crops, especially dairy products and beef.

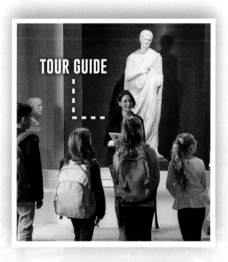

TOUR GUIDE

FARMER FEEDING COWS

19

CRICKET

Cricket has long been considered England's national sport. It is a little like baseball, with a bat, ball, and bases called wickets. *Football*, or soccer, has become more popular than cricket in recent years. The most famous English football clubs, or teams, are Liverpool, Arsenal, Chelsea, and Manchester United. English football fans are very loyal to their teams.

MANCHESTER UNITED

When not watching football games and other shows on the "telly," English people enjoy gardening, walking, swimming, and playing tennis. The **international** tennis tournament, Wimbledon, happens in London each summer.

WIMBLEDON

CONKERS

Conkers are made from horse chestnut seeds. Prickly green pods conceal seeds inside. For this activity, collect them from the ground around trees.

How to Make:

1. Ask an adult to help you make your conker. Start by preheating the oven to 475 degrees Fahrenheit (246 degrees Celsius).

2. Break open the horse chestnuts and choose a round, smooth seed.

3. Soak the seed in a 1/2 cup of vinegar for two minutes exactly (use a timer), then remove.

4. Put the seed in the oven for 1 1/2 minutes. Place on a counter to cool.

5. When it is cool, pierce a hole through the seed, and run a 1-foot (30-centimeter) long string through it. Tie a knot at one end so the seed dangles. That is your conker!

6. To play, hold your conker perfectly still and straight out in front of you. Your opponent has three tries to hit your conker with theirs. The first conker to be smashed is the loser. Be careful with your aim and how hard you swing. Bruised knuckles are a conkers side effect!

The English drink tea morning, noon, and night. It has become tradition to have "elevenses," a mid-morning cup of tea, as well as a mid-afternoon break. Sometimes afternoon tea is a large spread with sandwiches, cakes, and sweets.

English food is simple and hearty. Cottage pie has meat and vegetables topped with a mashed potato crust. Cornish pasties are filled sandwich pockets. A "full English breakfast," which the Brits also call a fry-up, has eggs, bacon, sausage, fried bread, mushrooms, beans, and tomatoes. Fish and chips are a popular takeout food. Indian food, introduced by immigrants, is also a favorite.

COTTAGE PIE

CORNISH PASTY

FISH AND CHIPS

MICROWAVE FLAPJACK RECIPE

A flapjack in England is a type of cereal bar or oatmeal bar. This gets hot! Have an adult supervise.

Ingredients:

1/3 cup butter

1/3 cup light brown sugar

2 tablespoons light corn syrup or honey

2/3 cup quick-cooking rolled oats

1/4 cup raisins

1/2 cup other dried fruit, chocolate chips, or whatever you like!

Steps:

1. Grease an 8x8-inch glass baking dish.

2. Place the butter, sugar, and syrup in a microwave-safe bowl. Microwave on high power for 1 to 2 minutes, or until butter is melted.

3. Stir in the oats, raisins, and other fruit or chips and mix thoroughly.

4. Press mixture into the baking dish. Cook on high power for about 4 minutes or until the center is bubbling. Allow to cool, then cut into squares. Makes 12 squares.

History inspires many English celebrations. The Trooping the Colour parade is held in London each June. It has celebrated the birthday of the **sovereign** for more than 200 years. Members of the Household Division march to Buckingham Palace in their red coats and bearskin hats. November 5 is Bonfire Night. Cities light bonfires and fireworks.

Boxing Day is December 26. The day got its name because servants received their gifts after working on Christmas Day. Now it is a day to spend with friends. It is another way England turns tradition and history into modern-day fun!

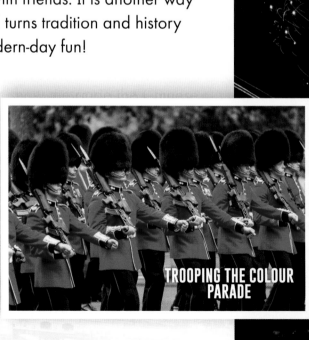

TROOPING THE COLOUR PARADE

WHO WAS GUY FAWKES?

Guy Fawkes and friends planned the Gunpowder Plot of 1605. They planned to blow up English Parliament and King James I. When Guy was caught, King James encouraged bonfires in celebration. This became Bonfire Night.

BONFIRE NIGHT

25

1558
Elizabeth I becomes queen and helps establish England as a world power

BEFORE 1000 AD
The Romans, Saxons, and Vikings invade England and fight for control

1066
William of Normandy conquers England at the Battle of Hastings and becomes the first Norman king of England

1215
King John signs the Magna Carta, limiting his power and promising people individual rights

2016

The British people vote for Britain to leave the European Union in a vote called Brexit

1707

England, Scotland, and Wales join together to form the Kingdom of Great Britain

1940

Germany's air force bombs London and the English countryside during World War II

1783

King George III accepts the United States of America as a separate nation, two years after the British army surrendered to George Washington

1914-1918

About 6 million Englishmen serve in World War I

2017

Queen Elizabeth II is the first British monarch to celebrate a Sapphire Jubilee, marking 65 years on the throne

ENGLAND FACTS

Official Name: England

Flag of England: A red cross centered on a white background. This is the cross of St. George, the patron saint and protector of England.

Area: 50,302 square miles
(130,281 kilometers)

Capital City: London

Important Cities: Manchester, Birmingham, Liverpool, Leeds

Population:
54,786,300 (July 2016)

WHERE PEOPLE LIVE

COUNTRYSIDE
17%

CITY
83%

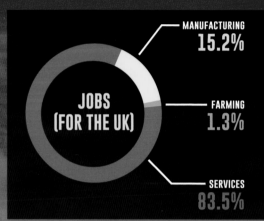

MANUFACTURING
15.2%

**JOBS
(FOR THE UK)**

FARMING
1.3%

SERVICES
83.5%

Main Exports (for the UK):

fuels

food

chemicals

beverages

tobacco

cars

National Holiday:
St. George's Day (April 23)

Main Language:
English

Form of Government:
constitutional monarchy

Title for Country Leaders:
prime minister (head of government),
queen (head of state)

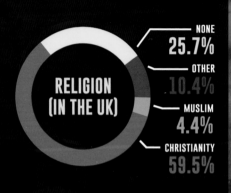

**RELIGION
(IN THE UK)**

NONE
25.7%

OTHER
10.4%

MUSLIM
4.4%

CHRISTIANITY
59.5%

Unit of Money:
Pound Sterling; 100 pence make up a pound.

GLOSSARY

accents—different ways to pronounce a language's words, based on location

apprenticeships—training positions during which a person learns a job or art from very skilled workers

dialects—local ways of speaking particular languages

hedgerows—rows of shrubs or trees that separate fields

hemispheres—halves of the earth, divided by the equator or prime meridian

immigrants—people who move to a new country

international—related to many different countries

mainland—a continent or main part of a continent

moors—areas of open, wet land unsuitable for farming

plains—large areas of flat land

punctuality—being on time

queuing—standing in line

reserved—cautious in words and actions

service jobs—jobs that perform tasks for people or businesses

sovereign—the highest ruler of a country; in England, the sovereign is not involved in the daily government of the country.

terrain—surface features of an area of land

tourism—the business of people traveling to visit other places

tradition—a custom, idea, or belief handed down from one generation to the next

TO LEARN MORE

AT THE LIBRARY

Banting, Erinn. *England: The Land*. New York, N.Y.: Crabtree Pub., 2012.

Banting, Erinn. *England: The People*. New York, N.Y.: Crabtree Pub., 2012.

Fuller, Barbara. *Great Britain*. New York, N.Y.: Cavendish Square Publishing, 2016.

ON THE WEB

Learning more about England is as easy as 1, 2, 3.

1. Go to www.factsurfer.com.

2. Enter "England" into the search box.

3. Click the "Surf" button and you will see a list of related web sites.

With factsurfer.com, finding more information is just a click away.

INDEX

The images in this book are reproduced through the courtesy of: Michal Bednarek, front cover, p. 9 (inset); Vika Suh, front cover (flag), p. 28 (flag); Alan Bauman, pp. 4-5, 14, 16-17, 23 (top middle); Juan Martinez, pp. 5 (top), 10 (top), 15 (bottom), 29 (coin); Travel Light, p. 5 (middle top); Patryk Kosmider, p. 5 (middle bottom); Kanuman, p. 5 (bottom); AridOcean, pp. 6-7, 8 (top); Justin Kase z12z/ Alamy Stock Photo, p. 8; Michael Conrad, p. 9; Andrew Michael/ Age Fotostock, pp. 10-11; Sue Robinson, p. 10 (middle top); Ramon Harkema, p. 10 (middle bottom); Sandra Standbridge, p. 10 (bottom); Mark Bridger, p. 10 (bottom corner); William Perugini, p. 12; dpa picture alliance archive/ Alamy Stock Photo, p. 13 (top); Julius Kielaitis, p. 13 (bottom); Katie Leaf, p. 15 (top); Jacky Chapman/ Alamy Stock Photo, p. 18 (top); Monkey Business Images, p. 19 (top); Peter Cade, p. 19 (bottom); Mitch Gunn, p. 20 (top); Jaggat Rashidi, p. 20 (bottom); Lucy Clark, p. 21 (top); Marilyn Barbone, p. 21 (bottom); OOK Die Bildagentur der Fotografen GmbH/ Alamy Stock Photo, p. 22; Joe Gough, p. 23 (top); BonChan, p. 23 (top bottom); Adam Edwards, p. 23 (bottom); ImageFlow, p. 24; Steve Allen, pp. 24-25; Durova, p. 26 (top); North Wind Picture Archives/ Alamy Stock Photo, p. 26 (bottom); Featureflash Photo Agency, p. 27; Various-Everythings, p. 28 (flag).